D1743262

Wildling

Wildling

© Kerry Sharpe, 2022

All rights reserved. No part of this book may be reproduced or transmitted in any form, by any means, electronic or mechanical, including a photocopy, recording, or any information retrieval system without the express permission of the author.

Cover art designed by Eliza Neilande, 2020. Used with permission of the artist.

ISBN: 978-1-6671-5775-7

Publisher: Lulu.com

Published and printed in the United Kingdom

This book

is not dedicated to you.

Origins

Where
do your roots
begin?

beneath stone

soil-work

shivering stars?

I am all three
& homesick.

Anxiety In Your Thirties

After you had spoken it
vomited it out
etched North
into your wrists

you ghosted your breaths
in white-whisped lungs,
echoing Sunday cappuccinos
that took the place of everything
troubling in life

you didn't want to be rude
but you couldn't help it

you didn't pause
saying goodbye
because truth
was a poem burning
a hole in your shirt pocket

and they didn't deserve
that wound

or any scar
long since hidden
beneath fear
& shirt sleeves.

You're never sure
why they left you
such useless roadmaps
but there you were
trying to make sense
of those coloured lines

somewhere in a loss
of absent
sleep

those long
silent
drives.

How To Be Empty

Remember
the gong that sounded
your arrival into this world,
bare and screaming, echoing
the wild cave you escaped

allow now a clear bell of dark
to match your steady heart,
embrace the welcome hum
of silent things beneath
that rhythm of love

ask not what is important,
but invite the question
of what makes you whole
in that unfiltered answer
of being.

When The Storm Breaks

Woman
take a bow—

    take another

it feels powerful
doesn't it?

    try it naked

step out
barefoot
on to grass

just you

    all of you

beneath
these stars

this sky

    this love.

Dear Will

Enough
of the daffodils, Sir

it's been done to death,
lifting green needle necks
to play Jerusalem through
gramophone heads

peeking proudly through
the fresh spring grass
on majestic hilltops
while choirs chirp
arias to leaves

and growth

and the wanton lustre
of gold glow under
a high-noon sun.

Dazzle me
with simple grace,
but never fool me
with mediocrity.

Write me
a pure thing, darling,
embrace the white silk
of root weaving hands
beneath sobering soil

unearth me,
but never own me
my happiness, or my stature

writing at the surface
the way God intends poems

before men and their old books
bury them alive.

Womb

English rain
drums windows
with damp sticks

the sky
is spilling water
and I am
shedding blood

and somehow, we
are both releasing
what no longer
serves us

breathing out
a universal
heartbeat

gifting our
tears

knowing our
song.

Dear Virus

You didn't tell us why you were doing this,
I found that a little rude

as you casually walked into the house
sat yourself down at the kitchen table
stole all of the pasta
and the good biscuits.

You didn't tell us why
you were doing this

in the middle of summer
when everything is in bloom
and we were hours just
hidden away

then you began to speak

you told me about time
and all the things that I
am yet to learn

you told me that you
have bought me home
to be close to myself,
to feel in my guts
the absence of people
I love

to appreciate
every
single
moment

that I have with them.

You told me about my old guitar
and journals full of stories,
you showed me book titles
and highlighted paragraphs
kept for emergencies
such as this

then you showed me my life
of those first tastes of glory felt
when reading a poem
or sitting out in the yard
under the ash tree
as I sang to the dawn

and you told me
not to hate you,
but to learn from you

something painful and pure
something vulnerable
that will break down fences
that will splash these beige walls
with colour and meaning

where there is no sickness
but joy screaming from
the rooftops of my
beating lungs
you told me

that you are not
who I thought you were
as you slide a blue mask
across the table

and slowly disappear
behind the peace
of a locked door.

Pisces

Sometimes
I trick
myself
into
this
belief
that
I am a
terrible
human
being
then
convince
others
I am
nothing
but a
raging
bitter
wave.

On Ivy

It doesn't
just grow

it consumes
everything
that it touches

attaches itself
to fences, trees,
climbing upward
outward

until whole spaces
become smothered.

Sometimes
it takes a morning
tearing vines
from old wood to put
things in perspective

you claw and pull
to rip a space free
from a death grip.

People.

People
can be ivy, too.

Human

Your rubble
tastes of
truth

I always
liked that
in a wreck

Falling Down

He'd lost his wife, kids
dignity disappearing into the wind
like gunshots and Sunday mornings

you watched with intent
that point-blank gym bag

white noise drowning out
the chaos of the street
across the square

I wondered if you knew
how bad it didn't have to be
as you lost yourself in a chair.

We're Expecting A Baby

...not a velociraptor
or a machine-gun wielding
minotaur in a belly labyrinth?

not a seven-pound pudding
swirling its way through
a thick sauce?

or a cabbage stuffed
under your jumper
you joked about
at sixteen,
twenty-one

when melon-balling
seemed impossible.

It was never
really a surprise
was it

that life developed
just like it was supposed to
in the midst of pink balloons
blue confetti

little white shoes hung
upon vacant
nursery doors.

Heathen Love Song

Misspelled words
vowels he never intends to keep
the dry burn of sanguine wine
when sky has barely drunk sun
the toying of age on a pivot
a laugh at the inappropriate,
the Devil in your smile

a carefully folded napkin
in the corner of a forgotten drawer
red, oceans of unforgiving scarlet
flooding the air in arias of change
the bended lamplight on your face
a taught skin of confusion
mapping a slow drive

I lay lilies
on the tombs of your throat
trap my prayers in layers of hair
that defines chaos
at its most beautiful,
and in your homelessness
you nidificate my love.

On Paganism

Laundry always
smells better
with the scent
of the wind

same goes
for people.

Solstice

And I have opened
my glowing palms
to pray before light,
a communion
of cupped hands
as the world sleeps
and the gentle thrum
of rapture strikes
a genesis of being.

Here is where
the answers come

not in lawless feet,
but in the steady beat of drum,
in the piercing wail of horn
shaking bones beneath
the tumbling stars.

I place trembling fingers
upon aching rock
and feel the old ways
curl my lips around
their tongues of lark

the sky
pouring libations
into a blood-red bay
inside the dark hum
of dreaming.

I've Been Thinking About Whittling

... to be specific

carving out a body
from supple linden,
thinking of torsos
as branches
long after a knife
aligns

I've been thinking
about whittling

dry old bones
from ancient woods,
giant femurs of pine
splintering from trunks
below the surface
waiting to be found

I've been thinking
about whittling

because
skin is grained,
a work in progress
I chisel and turn
until shapes form
beneath a blade

peeling back
and further still
until white again

clean.

Everyday Magic

It doesn't play a pompous fanfare
or marches around our estate
it doesn't proclaim its arrival
swinging open our garden gate

it isn't spells or incantations
it isn't witchcraft in a jar,
it doesn't practice Scientology
like some fancy-pants film star

it enters still and slowly,
it does not demand a throne,
it is humble in the backyard
where our vegetables are grown

it is blossom on our plum tree,
blackbirds on an old church spire,
it is your hand, soft on top of mine
as a log burns on our fire

it is bread baked in our oven
swelling up from kneaded dough,
it is eating toast by candlelight
beneath a worn-out woollen throw

for I believe in everyday magic
as the wild just passes through,
no secrets, no revelations
simply me, and simply you.

Woman, Sleeping

Your pen held your fear
in times when loneliness, a terror
kissed your children, your history
you feared would be taken from you,
you tapped into anguish, you knew
its language, the landscape of such

you tasted the plate glass hidden
in English words, polite and warmed
you traced the geometry of lines
on her face, morning white porcelain
light sheets and serenades of love
you collected them between
her fingers, you knew they were yours.

It was your holy place, your fracture
the sudden crescendo of Sunday
immediate and eternally beating
your furrows dressed in clinging light,
her sleep shrouded in conclusions
illuminations framed on pages clean
of dreams they stole from you.

Meanwhile In Jurassic Park

A child
screamed
so loudly
I considered
throwing
it a steak
to see if
it was part
dinosaur

*I mean
that kid erupted*

flailing its arms
with blunt hooks
latching on
to blue bags
of crisps whilst
Mumma dino
opened a text
and tried not
to shit an egg
in aisle two

because
across a tannoy
at that moment
a car rolled
from its space
and crashed
into a tree
while the
pterodactyls
outside

laughed

as I
questioned
the notion
of foraging
for pot noodles
in a pandemic
while nobody's
noticing at all
that second
Mesozoic
wave

and I'm just
not feeling like
facing a fucking
tyrannosaurus
today.

Diagnosis

They tell me
there's blue in you, my girl

there are seas in your chest
and waves in your mouth

water in your eye lids,
black pupil shaped boats

as pills slide across counters
in ill-fitting life jackets.

They say if I swallow
the ocean will come back for me.

Leave A Light On

Orange teak cabin in the rain
decking soaked to the skin
as sheep walk sideways
seeking shelter under branches

I do the same under a veranda
a cup of chai in one hand,
a red pen in another
while he reads words already written
and I write new ones beneath mist
overlooking an old graveyard
with crumbling tombs.

I sauntered there earlier
unearthing graves from 1593
buried beneath winter catkins.

These are
my favourite places to explore,
to get wet feet amongst bones sleeping
as magpies swoop from tree to tree,
their omens impenetrable through briars.

The chapel faced a mountain,
it felt poignant somehow—
to be buried at the foot of sky
waiting for clouds to clear.

On my return, dark descended—
the dirt track draped in twilight,
fire flickered in a distant window
glowing against our woodshed roof

I inhaled the incense of old birch burning

silver paper licking scented flame
back to the comfort of my everyday mug,
back to he who shares my name.

Hymn To Herne

How dreamlike was your human form,
your lichen hair so slick with dew,
the crows made nests out of your eyes
as rabbits wombed the breath of you

I knew you were a wayward God
the snakes upon your throat, their sighs
the wren, he chattered 'neath your horns
into onyx spirals of my eyes:

Where there is shadow, there ye find
the cloven foot of beast abound
and through the silence of the trees
the Otherworld sings underground

though we dance, though we embrace
through galaxies within our stare,
you are the dark lord of the hunt—
I'll meet you in the wild wood there.

The Black Morris

Samhain torches
roar through darkness
as you realise you
are not ready

you are unprepared
for bone rattles
draped in
black threads

to meet night
in all her glory
marking an end to all
you know of this world.

Why have you come?

What is it
that is undoing you
before that ancient call
of mouth and drum

beating holy flowers
in a church
market square

parishioners melting
into petals—

because this dance
does not want anything
from you

it is you

standing
before another voice
you have not allowed
to speak.

On Prayer

To pray
with the hands

respectable

to pray
with the feet

divine.

Cycle

Soon
my womb
will bloom

latching on
to life with
sticky hands

and my body
will swell
with purgatory

never knowing
which of us
is more desperate.

All I Know Of Love And Letting Go

There's a sense
of achievement
that comes
from doing it
yourself

the more
I think about that
I never felt it once
the whole time
I did it for you.

Samson

In the May breeze
my uncut hair
brushes my cheek

it feels like your hand

I'm not ready to let go
of that just yet.

.45

I've been rattling
a God lotto

guess I never was
a full house

Keep Some Room In Your Heart For The Old Ways

When you are a child
learning is about success

it's how you grow
fully committed to your art,
those gold stars & trophies
lined up on a shelf.

When you become older
you embrace worldly insanity
finding words in torn bandages,
discovering your poem

and it becomes less
about achievement—
more a matter of survival
processing your thoughts
beyond sticky wounds
into something pure.

As you grew, your parents
would have never dreamed
of putting excellence
above happiness

yet here you are
romanticising your demons
as though they are one path
to an ink-stained existence,
those ghosts of syntax
keeping you awake
long into the night.

I look to the bards

as ancestral lighthouses

those oral traditions
teaching me more
than surface skin
earthing itself
in entitled humanity

they taught me not
to echo those mavericks,
that it is my responsibility
to ground myself—
to be practical

to own everything
I hold in this space
as absolute truth

scribed, with love
in my own bloodied
meaning.

Mythos

I shouldn't
have been surprised
that I couldn't write it down;
it made no rational sense
after all

yet

I remember reading
those wise ones
never shelved
a damn thing.

There was
some reason
in this—

you can't stop
rivers from flowing
through empty valleys

and so it is
with mystery.

Henge

Crown of moss
& ancient doors

inside a cathedral
her belly —

life is birthed
in rhythmic awe

divinity
beating.

Stepping The Boards

In the morning
where blood
is only a song
of lark

I fold myself
within your wings

paint your feathers
tipped in morning.

You remember
our dance
don't you—
those points
unseen

we'll tread the music
that lost us.

Doing Time

Saw a man
who carried
no photos
in his wallet

I admired
the bravery
of it

setting free
a dog
a wife

& kids.

Prophecy

and I dreamed
that the whole world
was a dark crystal
laced on a black string

hung from my throat
where all prayers linger

branches scratched in red
across a midnight sky,
white ash smouldering
above bedrock.

Almost Feelings

Your toes disruptive
kicking sleep
within a blue yawn,
breath beneath crumbs
and napkins never found

a belly full of morning
thumbing my notebook
in scattered words
spilling fear into a bowl
of anticipation

you pull a pen from your hair

I love you most then.

Arwen

A storm
washes
these
dirty
windows

cleaning
day at
the
Marie
Celeste.

Mono

I chose these tiles
from ninety shades
and all so I could say,
this house is mine
that I designed

a bathroom
in slate grey

and every time
this water beats
against my skin-tight day,
these squares are drops
inside my mind

a bathroom
in slate grey

for there's a sadness
inside [out]
that I cannot convey,
my eyes see walls
of every kind

a bathroom
in slate
grey.

Unanswered

How
long
is it
from
here
to
there

empty
space

eternal
death

how
long
dear
Gods
do I
have
left.

An Everyday Cup

It was
the simplicity of it

turning a tap clockwise
to the splutter and gush
of my unquenched thirst

each rivulet, a bead
of mala prayer
strung from a throat
made of waves.

It was a holy thing,
to hear northern Gods
chime their copper pipes
into glass bells

my tongue wet
with the dew
of a hundred
mornings

a thousand moments
of crystal stillness—

it tasted free
as if it had clawed
it's way through rock,
filtered through stone
upon heavy stone

reminding me
that everything

takes time.

Treasures

That night
I stood naked
before Orion

arms outstretched
reclaiming the words
witch & womanhood.

He silently nodded,
pointed towards Venus
and with bare knees
I sat quietly before her
glowing in the cosmos

her halo shimmering
through pine boughs
those trunks creaking;
bending back
in an echo of shadows

.

.

.

morning came
and honey grass
lay sweet with dew

took myself out
to gather birch logs,
walking a track
of littered gravel

it was there that I saw

three tail feathers
poking from the bank
as I slowly pulled them
from wet leaves
examining

.

.

.

it was a female pheasant
long brown plumage
stemming from needlepoints
rupturing from Earth
as if carefully placed

these were my gifts,
my trio of treasures
rising from dark soil
as they gently draped
over my sleeves

affirming themselves
Goddess

declaring me
one of their own.

Rinsey Cove Blues

13:30

high tide had rolled
across sunlight

rocks lay scattered,
sky dominoes
carelessly toppled
in submission
to something more.

My feet clambered
those uneven pathways
haphazardly carved
into a cliff face

toes hungry for cold waves
that would sate them.

As I paddled through wet sand
I looked back at fallen edges,
all puzzle pieces lying unclicked

my mind working silently
on a Monolithic jigsaw
to the sound
of children's laughter

buckets and spades
drumming nature
into sand-starved hands.

I couldn't let it go, this need
for everything to fit

in perfect synergy

as I dared to question
an illogical God

those giants
saying nothing

at all.

How Great Thou Art

Nothing encapsulated faith more
than flower rotas, finger cakes
served by frail kitchen dwellers
obedient to their Husbands
and their God,
that same hymnal

bellowed from chests
until heartbeats
swelled in worship.

There's a part of me
that loathes the pomp of it

rituals of laced teacups
hiding limp handshakes,
hollow sugared greetings
as a donation tray jingles

meanwhile
a memory is triggered
of intimacy—

not communion wine
or clean white smocks,
but a cause to sing out
from the heart in praise
of something more

I want every song
that leaves my lips
to be a victory tune,
a melody of hope

that rouses from
the start—

how great thou art

     how great
     thou art.

House Box

There's a weave in this blanket
I cannot consciously repeat—
a complex interlocking
of left over right

blue meeting white
in repetitive waves

so to, wind drafts
through deft branches,
over the quarry stone
into the pine-flocked sails
of this moss-covered home

a fire is lit in an overture
of wool and storm
and outside, black enters
threading itself into tapestries
of flame and star

you sleep soundly in a chair,
a rattan rug at your feet
and I look at you from an old bed
through a drapery of love.

A Charge Of Shadows

There's something about sunset
that demands action

as we light our candles,
gather logs and kindling
settling down with kettles
on a burning stove

we hoard matches,
barricade the doors
from English weather,
thinking ourselves lucky
as rain drums against tin.

As nature moves
we move with her

judging her breath,
her every song
until night becomes
a seamless act
of synchronicity

and here is where Heaven
meets Earth, this daily dance
of twinset shadows
in a rush of dawn

those gifts of perfect
dark.

Journaling

Jaw wakes me first, a pincushion
in the side of the bed.

It was strange waking here
in the midst of oak beams,
solid quarry slate made home
wedged in the middle
of televisions, a microwave.

It's six in the morning

brew number four
is already being drunk
while my sisters snore
above me

I can't help but think
about all the stories
lingering here

divided into separate rooms,
different chapters of life

and it seems to me
that living writes itself
in amongst rough drafts
and masterpieces

verses written,
tales journaled as we slip
into ancient myth

the way
of these mist-covered lands.

Victoria Plum

It's been 3 years you've been gone

3 years of sleeping quietly
enough to know all answers
and nothing at all.

I come to you
because I too need God
within this chaos
and you bloom quietly
between shed and fence

your flowers
a white child of spring.

I sat here when she passed too

gave that fear to the Universe

asked not for what I wanted
but what was best for her,
living being

her

sentient stars filled with the love
of thousands.

It is dawn
as I hear the blackbird's song
from a roof top cathedral
and all of her is alive
in some morning
some form.

Sunday Mornings

Stones are
the tears of a God
forced to stay
in one place.

Carita

In my sleep
you wander through
the wild mallow

slashing dark pods
with a golden
scythe

watering your dead
with your last cry
of alive.

Funeral

There are black flies
caught in a silver web
above the door.

A spider wraps
the sticky bodies
in methodical silk
and I say a prayer
to the dead —

I know what it is
to be bound

to be helpless,
at the mercy
of mouths

to tear off dreams
like wings.

To A Nobody

I've walked miles today

my body feels it,
it is raw and it is silent
and in that nausea
my blood filters
through sentry rock

I fill my bones with it
this tenacious soup,
determined

to sate a hunger

this

    hunger...

for a moment, I think back
to the starvation of your love
an ancient moss-drenched jungle
as I bow before the nature
of wildness

it echoes claustrophobia
against sleepless eyes
and the howling of old lungs
with no earthly place to go

    I forgive you, you know.

Northern Skies

I have awoken
to the sound
of a thousand giants
rattling my teeth

I wish them no harm,
but there is urgency
in their ritual
I refuse to deny.

Tell me, Pilgrim
the miracles you lay
before my hungry knees

where I await
in Godless space,
those stars dripping
their foreboding sighs—

I dedicate myself
to these Northern skies

so too, I rise

so too, I rise.

Old Demdike

She knows how horizons shiver
before shoes are thrown
children scowling
through lamplight.

She knows
the weight of clay effigies
beneath boards, pocked skin
amongst howling gorse

Her, trapping air
in clay pots
knees jangling
like rusted pins.

The fear of blood leaving a body
seeping madness into marshland,
the low swoop of foxglove tongues

          she feels that pain—

blue stars earthing her body
and her ears feral mushrooms
bursting through the moon.

On Sundays she whittles the wild
into laddered knots, carving
tallies into hand-gathered grains

that's a penny a spell, she says
won't you mind the daisy chains.

Welcome The Wonderful

Too many people
are afraid to piss
outside

**God's seen your ass
a thousand times.**

Tambourine Whackers Of The World Unite

Occasionally I like to torture myself
by visiting the visceral scourge
that is Ladbible.

Why would you do that I hear you cry?
I'm glad you asked fellow confused human
because sometimes I like to read
the most outrageous article I can find
then read the comments to view
how society really functions.

There was an article posted today
about the spiritual arty-fartyness
of women who participate
in new-age practices.

I open the comments
and begin to read

*"I bet you right she's a cross-fitting vegan
who vapes, has an intolerance to gluten
and hasn't shaved her pits in two years"*

states one.

*"I bet you she's called dancing-rain
and uses a menstrual cup and owns
fifteen cats and weaves ponchos"*

said another

but my favourite was this:

"Those fucking tambourine whackers right,

I can't stand those happy wankers
stinking out the place".

We now live in a world
where happiness is mocked,
because we've chosen to try.

A little background information:
I own seven decks of inspirational cards,
charge my crystals under the full moon
and once didn't shave for so long
I had a bush like Bob Marley's afro.

I walk bare feet when it's been raining,
I get up every solstice and equinox morn
and play my drum for the land at sunrise
while the houses below still sleep
and the wheat fields dance.

I burn mugwort instead of sage
to cleanse my rooms and hearth
because it is an indigenous plant
to the ancestors of Avalon.

People ask me why I burn
such a potent herb in my house
and I tell them if you don't want
to enter my doorway because
you can't stand the smell,
it means

the mugwort

is working.

Why do I do all this?

because I'm a tambourine whacker, baby
and if it is against the ways of modern life
to try and find a little happiness,
if it is beyond the pale of existence
to stride out into the unknown,
to plunge my fists into the beating heart
of art and poetry and all that is good
in this unforgiving world

I'd rather be musical.

I'd rather make some noise.

I'd rather grow my hair down
to my bare bellybutton
and remember how it feels
to dance naked around a fire,
to not worry about my body
my flushed cheeks
the grey in my hair

I'd rather my sisters build me up
at a time where we are made to feel
inadequate, self-absorbed
in all ways designed to shield us
from the magic we are missing,
when we were never meant to be
a match-head flickering

we were made to be lighthouses
vibrant Milky Ways—
atomic bombs

and we were made for more—
more than this 9-5 routine,

more than spending forty pounds
to have our eyebrows match

more than boxes the miserable people
pack us away in to keep us small
because they can see we smile

and it terrifies them
because their bells are rusted

their ribbons are torn

they don't hear the music
that spins this globe
with meaning.

We Grew Sunflowers, You And I

You dug into the shallows
and I salvaged large pots
as we watched the tendrils
curl thick stems with magic

and they grew and grew
through worldly chaos,
despite August's burnt petals
echoing halos that glowed
at your birth.

I picked up the harvested seeds
in an old salsa jar on a shelf
and listened to the rattle of husks
clink their shells against the glass.
hearing ice cracking across a lake
where you once skated

how it stayed with me
in spite of everything,
this image of you free
and beating.

Always remember, my dear
that somewhere in the world
a garden is being tended

leaves are heading home,
the low swoop of willow
is undressing by the water

and I—

I promise

I will meet you there,
the dark suns growing
beyond Earth.

If You Need Arms, Boy

(For Ethan)

Your high noon
on which you weep
mutters something
about belonging

old cupboards,
broken hinges
creaking
their sentry blues

as you cocoon yourself
in familiar wool
spinning new wings
in the molten dark—

if you need arms, boy
if you cannot fly

allow me to carry
those raw wrists
down to the river

let these words
vessel your desolation
amongst a bruising swell

as certain as your eye
beneath hopeful
hands

as echoing
& infinite.

Of Star And Crescent

That moment
as if the whole of space
has lit up long enough
to never ask your name

arched back on a curb
in the middle of cars
and emerging
from blackness
is coal you
could never touch

but I see her halo
up there
and you tell me
you see her too
through smog

and after three weeks
of nothing I stare
into a ceaseless deep

thinking of how smiles
exist under bright lights
as I close a warm door.

That.

That feeling.

That's my star.

The Moon Is A Memory

I asked the moon
if she remembered me

as she lit up dark trees
in a quiet neighbourhood,
and I lit three candles
in her blanket dark.

I asked the moon
if she remembered me

she said
she knew me once,
but I was busy and tired
as she glimpsed my face
from a passing car,
a dim bathroom light

curtains anchored shut
as eyelids sailed for dawn.

I asked the moon
if she remembered me

she said she met me
on the day I was born
firing her stars
in my honour

she said she'd light
a thousand more
if I'd only
look up

allow

slow

    down.

I asked the moon
if she remembered me

and we talked for a while
through chimney pots
with open arms

in silent
space.

Birthing

There was something methodical
about lacing that drum,
a wheel of clockwise opposites
rotating its lineage in complex stars

skin isn't like rope,
it stretches—
did three rounds of gentle pulling
into long, thin guttural strands.

For a second, I dared to smell
the pile of death in front of me
as I was reminded of the cloying
scent of wet dog

I looked carefully at the hide
still seeing follicles, dark blemishes,
opaque patches where life existed

lay my hands on the strange wet whelk
laying limp before me.

For a second, I felt the beast alive,
its nose nuzzled against my forehead
breathing foreign comfort into my mind

pulled that elastic pelt tighter
and tighter, until it became
a living thing once more
adopting the ash hoop as bone
as I tied my trinkets into it,
silently nodding to my ancestors.

A room full of women lay on the ground

clutching new-borns above their wombs,
it seemed a haunting parallel of births

the umbilicals strung out,
placentas broke loose.

Words To Live By

When weight of the world
makes me weary
and I am held
a prisoner of youth,
I look to the sky
with open hands
and cry out

speak your truth

I guess it's not wine
or a razor
& it may seem a little
uncouth—
but these words,
they save me daily
as I whisper

speak your truth

I promise it's not
hipster trend-speak
or new-age babble
long in the tooth,
but a mantra
drumming through
silence

speak your truth

speak your truth.

Radical Acceptance

1.

Simplicity pours through the grates
and the splashes are bigger this time
echoing through the parlour walls

I have been floating
for a long time

drenched in the living
I fold my skin
into a paper vessel

sail love notes
deep into storm drains
and call them rafts

2.

I remember when the lights
burned my eyes in the dark

the match heads all gone
leaving nothing
but the nub

3.

If there are angels,
if God listens
to my musings,
if the crystals are
in any way correct

they chart
my spinning bones
to the northern star:

home begins exactly
where you
are.

Shuvihani

One morning, you awoke
with the sting of your lungs
beating a need

you felt it in your spine,
your aching womb space

it was ancient and familiar,
it did not know your humble ways,
stamped into the hallway
demanding tea and warmth
from your fire

it sat at your table
asking you your name
and you reply the same letters
you've whispered since birth

but it refuses your vowels,
your wounded consonants

instead, it takes a knife
from your well-stocked drawer,
carves a lost word into a tree
as your fingers cry out
at the shape of remembering.

You remember ancestral trails
of bare feet and blankets,
you remember those tinctures
harvested from overgrown lanes

but mostly,
you remember who you were

before your children needed feeding,
before your house consumed you,
before bills needed to be paid

you are a daughter, Shuvihani
of every woman before you

wagon trails rattling
your feral, sacred bones.

On Rebirth

Give a man
an axe and he
will chop down
the waiting woods

hands then
make matches
pencils & picks.

I am surrounded
by grand gestures
made meaningless—

failure,
a whittled spoon

God,
an open blade.

The Return Of Cousin Itt

I was never sure
what made a woman
stop shaving

or throw her razor
in the bin until
she could play
her pubes like
a harp—

I've got
Viking pits now

and I've come to like
this underarm beard
pillaging my body.

It's an experiment
of course,
I fiddle from time
to time

but apparently, I can
reclaim my body hair
& re-write the rules
of womanhood

though it seems
people would rather
shit on a puppy
than deal with
the legs of a gibbon

as though lockdown

taught us nothing
about how much crap
we've been fed

regarding waxing
and pruning

to satisfy nobody
leaving us
passive-aggressive
tweezers at our door.

Land Of Giants

I'm concentrating on my phone
as I open a public restroom door
almost knocking over a child
who barely reaches my knee

she's a gorgeous little Asian girl—
huge demerara eyes that peer out
beneath pink-bowed pigtails,
clutching an orange juice box
with both hands.

For a moment
we look at each other

her fruity drink in tiny paws,
my microchips under thumbs
as she suddenly realises
her parent isn't me
and she starts to panic
looking for a protector,
gazing upwards at cubicles
as she whimpers through a straw.

Soon her mother opens a door
scooping her up in her arms
as they laugh under the hand drier
with her pig tails blowing back
in little tousled flags.

Even as a grownup,
when things go wrong
we react in the same way
as we stand there searching
for someone of wisdom—

a more *adultier* adult
to hold our hands,
make us belly laugh

all of us looking for giants
in an ordinary world.

Prayer To Sulis

Where I am incomplete,
may oceans cleanse
my heartsick sighs

where I am lost,
wandering lone cliff tops
may cobalt be ever shown

where I am arid,
let my cup be always filled
within chalices of my eyes

where you exist,
bare youthful maiden
so too, the watchful crone.

Blood Song

There's blood soaking
black cotton

flowing legs
& dark streets
into rivers and drains

it's on my fingers
as I touch lamps
post-boxes
phone booths

I cannot escape
her artistry
painting everything
on the news

blood red in the living
    red blood on the dead.

On Poetry

The trouble is
you are always
striving for words
you think are more
beautiful than
yourself.

Joseph

It started with a woman
as things so often do
Mary comes home and says
my love... I've got something to tell you

and she takes off her cloak
washes her hands, fiddles
with dinner and
the pots and pans

and says *"Joseph I'm pregnant...*
now hear me out if you can,
I, I didn't sleep with another bloke
this here's the Son of man"

he didn't say anything
just acted forlorn
found his dear one a barn
& watched that child be born

and this is the story
that started the fate
of how men can hide all
that they have on their plate.

Women are coming together
to talk cycles & their power
but I can't help but look at him
wishing he'd grasp the hour

and speak to other fellas
who know the dark pain
of mistrust and betrayal
as they walk in the rain

but this isn't the end
yes — us women are zealous
but I wish that they'd join us
instead of feeling jealous

it's not all mad feminism
and wild yoga poses
but an outpouring of truth
in front of our noses

you aren't alone, oh no
there are millions of brothers
but if you never speak out,
you'll never find the others

and part of me wonders
beneath bravado's song
if they're really that brave,
if they're really that strong

then I open the news
and hear headlines say
sixteen men end their lives
every
single
day.

And what of my Joseph
he sits blank in half-light
as I watch his thoughts drain him
until he can no longer fight

but he brings home our bread
and this house I do clean,
and he's still the most beautiful wreck

I've ever seen

and Joseph has a secret
that rings warning bells inside
our men told us they were invincible—

I guess those chests, they lied.

What I Want To Say To All Black Lives

nothing

I wouldn't *say*
a goddamn
thing

I'd listen

and therein
lies the difference.

Walk Into The Arena

The first time I felt real fear
everything changed

I was eleven and riding a bike
with a girl I'd known forever
in the way all rural kids do
riding for miles through lanes
that wound their tangled tracks
around neighbourhood farms

we caught the gaze of local boys
who began to chase us through trees
throwing stones at our wheels.

We rode
as fast as legs would stride
over the wooden bridge
down the sycamore hill
faster

     faster

until the spokes
skidded.

I was thrown from the bike,
my head colliding with the force
of a mud wall
knees bleeding
hands impacted with gravel,
crash helmet cracked in two.

Took me a while
to get back on the bike,

but kids are resilient—

within a few months
I missed peddling around
the old dairy yard,
past the water pump
guarding the witches house
(or so people said)

If there's one thing I learned
from that day, it's that
I loved freedom more
than fear.

Years later
I found myself standing before
a small crowd of women
performing a poem
feeling vomit rise from guts,
my bare-feet quaking
against the carpet

but I kept reading
body electric
eager in its message,
burning with the magic
of the microphone
visualising her death,
his accusatory hands
everything

that had led me
to this moment,
this breath
this
longing

to move beyond.

Fear
is a piss-poor excuse
for anything

because all we have to do
to beat it is to show up—
to keep showing up

stomach churning
heart pounding
palms moist
in the lamplight

and we do this
because fear is the only thing
that makes us feel truly alive.

I want to wake up every morning
and feel my knees shake their bells
to the tune of my potential,
my eyes stinging with the whiplash
that lies between nightmares & awake
and I want to live

I want to live so bad
that my pills shake in their packets,
that death will take one look at me
and realise it can't kill a storm

and I can only do this
if I keep showing up
setting light to anxiety

head held high
walking into the arena

because you never know
how fucking good
that grass looks
beating your fists
against the walls

outside.

Ashes

That's all
that was left,
a purgatorial bowl
bottling a mind.

I couldn't fathom
why they'd bury
existential remains

then I wondered
how many deaths
I'd swallowed
mid-air.

Sacrifice

Trees
give their bodies
to make the axe
that kills them

& I can think
of no simpler way
to explain
this life.

Psalm Of The Non-Believer

They say that hospital walls
have heard more prayers
than empty church beams.

I'm not sure
if atheists pray,
but I am half-God

and listening.

Closing Time

Your death came as no surprise
it had raged for quite some time,
but the world had you buried
the same day you measured him
for his Earth bed

you never forgot
how it felt to lay in wait

and lay you did, while a woman cried
over your all-consuming blackness,
her hands clasped in daily prayer
as she asked for an exit sign.

I know my absence spoke volumes
and as the thunder over the hills
rolled in from a quiet place
I considered the metaphor
remembering my recurring dream
of a stag walking into a silent church

suddenly, the lightning cracked a whip
and the poetry that followed frightened me
under its dome of claustrophobic grief

that hollow,
primal cave.

Daily Bread

For a moment
everything was circular

wheat became corn
grain became seed
under tillage of soil,
unbreathing

yet
stretching prevailed
in skyward shoots

it felt more like a prayer
this way:

dough became glutinous
and with outstretched arms
I nurtured flour in rounds
witnessing a resurrection

dust became hair
oats, strange teeth.

Bigger Chests

Meaning:

somewhere
between a
cabbage and a
baby's head.

We could tell you
a thing or two
about backache

dresses that don't fit,
getting them caught
on the bathroom door

we wouldn't dare
run down the stairs
without a bra

it'd be a knockout.

First

The sheets were
the first thing to burn

we scrubbed out red
with old toothbrushes

felt feverish before those
shades of womanhood

imagined the implausibility
of cotton— how swelling

was the first of many problems
and we never paid attention

to the under-door books,
biology classes

because seeing it, seeing
that smear was silent

more than us, and nothing
on a quiet Monday morn.

There were no balloons
as skirts slid downwards

walking the packed paths
amongst dandelion blooms

our stained garments
in a dark laundry bag

traffic seeming louder
than before.

Nebula

Some nights
she is unsure
if she is imploding

exploding—

if she gives herself over
and often
to sticky hands canvassing
an arched throat with dust.

She is dancing in a body
too broken to be beautiful

look how her eyes weep

her chest detonating
amongst dark
mattered
things

come now
dear woman

look how
wounds
shine—

look how
blood
shatters
a dead
galaxy
with

stars.

Women Like Us

They told
women like us
to simmer down

because our rage
made us less
beautiful

but we pissed
all over those
matches—

our bodies,
feral bonfires

created
to burn.

What A Conundrum

Purchased
a poncho today
to cover
my naked ass
when changing
by the lake

yet I throw myself
into the water
with gay abandon
in a Lycra condom
without a thought
of poached eggs
on show

or white thighs
gleaming under
the sun.

Never been happier
to tread that fine line
between freedom
and disgrace.

The Quiet At The End Of The World

There are days
I lay ferns across
a hot chest
parallel to a heart

drink in
moist pine liquor;
swallow her down
to a mossed stomach

as I learn, humbly,
from yellow stagshorn
growing curiously
over dead wood.

It's easy enough
to be Pagan here,
to feel the old ways
howl at haunted trees

earthing a body
hung out for dead
in a place no more
dying than living

and I—

I'm not sure
I can leave her now,
she who whips cheeks
with a cold slash of wind

she who teaches me
to gaze silently out

across an iron tarn
in search of Herne

hammering
a spinal dulcimer
with two femurs
in wildling fists

a beast
made God
in the drumbeat
of knowing.

Everybody Writes Love Songs To The Living

I plant wet feet
in moorland dirt

pay my respects

to her;
noble cadaver
below a hum of crows

her grave
is a ghost

howling out across
peat tombs
weaving mournful music
through skeletal trees.

I know not why
the living write songs
to temporary flesh

what remains
is eternal

like the shrapnel
of wartime air crashes
scattering a hillside

the sheep skull
half-submerged
in an all consuming
earth

spines of slate walls

attached to rib fences
longing to be
remembered

adored.

30 Seconds

I wanted to write
something amazing
but instead, all I got down
on the page was this

a valuable lesson
that what matters in life
isn't fucking perfect
every time.

Anatomy Of A Poet

To the hours I wake
without the sting
of inspiration

I thank you—

those moments I cry out
to the flesh of existence,
when I am reduced to
a blindness of page

I come here
to dip my hands
in this blood

where fired ink
is never quenched

and if I cannot burn
I smoulder what is left
of my dreams upon
a pyre of books—

I know not why
I crumble

why I yearn.

On Disappointment

The yellow road
lead Dorothy
straight back
home.

Mileage

A map is the distance in miles
between two points of interest
built years ago, not existing
to please the next, but to be
a waypoint

delivering their hidden secrets
to waiting feet, reaching for it
searching for meaning
purging the land of skeletons
and stories meant to be lived
in the moment

the blood.

I close my eyes at the thought,
my guts wrenching
in their own silence

I too, am leaving.

I too have searched my way
through the dark.

I have packed up my bags
without warning, stuffed in
the odd socks, the pens,
the page

removed myself
from the body of Earth

those bones, faceless dead ends
I gifted to the adventurer if only

to remember me by

and I want so desperately
to lay that spade at your feet,
tell you to dig into the wet clay
and I can tell you about living,
how hard it was to breathe

how the air is so thin down here

but all you could do
is build your coffins in my throat,
sentence my body to tombs of shards

I listen to those words scream out
my heart burns with the fury of goodbye
and this city in which I loved you
crawls on its knees through glass
writing their terror on the streets
away from here

and maybe you did watch
beside the bins, beneath the stars
this story of decay, wrote triads
decorated in guiltless tinsel

made yourself feel useful,
more beautiful than your pitiful scar.

Odd Specifics

In the kitchen across spoons
you watch old game shows and I
look out over twilight gloom

I want to love you until I die
hold tears like warm peaches
until I'm carrying the moon

I pour tea, black, and feel young
the milk discarded in the fridge
echoing one more lost room.

Temple Mount

There's a blackbird
crying an old parable
across righteous trees

a shrine overturned
in the silver midst of
Sunday's plucked weeds

he sings of
gold over a palm,
a den of iron thieves

the church bells
strike three beyond
the cunning leaves.

The Space Between

I sit pressed against the fence
incense lit, a heady blend of sage
and sandalwood drifting through ivy
out, out into the waking world

she is in the yard again,
her lyrical Polish flooding through
the branches of overhanging ash

only the tree separates us
despite her love of barbecue
seasoned with the spices
of her mother tongue,
despite our parked cars
and their oddly coded plates

how she arrives at the door
for parcels and lost footballs
pointing her fingers while her mouth
speaks the questions only she hears

and I wonder if she too sees
dappled light caressing
the scented balm of flowers
across a wooden divide

I wonder if her words
are more beautiful.

The Broom Closet

not
content
with boxes

we made
circles.

Local Tales For Local People

Across a steel bridge
a white-washed tavern appeared
through blacked-out trees

built in the 1600's,
oak beams drank smoke
from a double log burner
cast-iron and sturdy,
as old as the walls.
Four men gathered round a square table,
their unruly beards stained with ale
playing dominos above golden retrievers

they talked of a bet made many years ago
regarding the recent freezing weather,
snow was noted in a farmer's almanac
which sat upon a dusty kitchen shelf.

I listened as I slowly ate,
their eyes burning the back of my neck
as I consumed their last portion of crumble
much to the disgust of old men, their dogs

rafters creaking
in the cold, Welsh air.

On Paper

I found my one good pencil
snapped in two beneath
the leg of the couch.
I'm sure this is a sign
the woman should
buy more pencils.

In fact
I sellotaped splintered wood
which is the biggest metaphor
for this year I can muster

but I let it slide
into a terrible film
and incense
and a mug of tea made
to make the world
step the hell down.

Drawing is not
something I share

it's a secret world of doodles
and etches, and flip-decks
of leaf variants all tied up
in a little book used
to observe the world

and you—
you were the first person
I ever sketched out, hair
being most important,
wild stars entering all
on their own.

Thought about many things
during that evening

how I've spent months
blocking everyone out,
how I can't handle people
the same as before

how hard it is to keep myself
fixed in one place

but not tonight—

tonight, I dwelled in the peace
of graphite things, in a way
never dreamed of
before you came

instead
I gently closed
the cover

my eyes.

Wedding Dress

The box was still
how I remembered it

I made it
after all

folded satin
down on itself,
tucked the laces
of an ivory corset
inside tissue sheets

traced my fingers
over tiara crystals
that flickered light
over the walls

and you—

you lay here too
wrapped within silk,
your hands upon
lace threads

you are in dust marks
on a wild underskirt
as we took that walk
beside a dark lake

stood beneath
an orb
intertwined.

Truth is I've tried

to immortalise it,
tried to pen down
all you mean

but I've never
been able to
write it down

because I cannot
trivialise your skin
with a rhyme

I cannot spill out
the faith on my tongue
that longs to confess
every beating star

neither
my dear
will I try—

there are thousands
of poems burning
within the temple
of an eye.

I Took The Day Off To Pray

to howl ecstatically at the moon;
to love myself unconditionally
before the adoration of thousands
on this Samhain night
scattering rosemary
at my feet

I took the day off to pray

to cocoon myself
in sorrow;
to open my mouth
and let grief spill out
like a dark spell I hold
in a pod of womb

I took the day off to pray

because
I am vulnerable
and sometimes afraid
as the world closes in
around me; as rain
pelts slate windows
against England's
tattered shroud.

I took
the day off
to pray

nothing more
nothing less—

it is humble
and inoffensive
because I am worthy
of mercy I sometimes
wholly fear to tread.

I build that altar
in my heart

my
head.

Fury

There was
this stallion once

kicked its front feet
off the ground

reared up on hind legs,
drunk spindles
chaotic

clouding
thick dust
into air.

Couldn't help
but see myself
there

backed
into a corner,
knotted hair
black eyed
heels
dug in
to Earth.

It made rage beautiful
in an unassuming way,
harnessed raw powers
of wild-born things

now
I allow myself
the repentance

of reckless grace

I strive
to make
fury
an art.

Black Nab Ghosts

Those great brass bells
ring through low mist,
old ruins shake
their spectres free

and those long dead
have gifted souls

to the sea
to the sea
to the sea.

Tumbling tombs
hold ancient bones,
black crows they rest
in every tree

they spread jet wings
to drift the winds

of the sea
of the sea
of the sea.

Palms are pressed
against cold stone
and in this moment,
only me

upon a clifftop's
rugged wilds

and the sea
and the sea

and the sea.

Lughnasadh

It's so delicate

the way
we call them
ears of corn

as if the fields
wait in wonder
to hear our thanks

our prayers.

On Peace & Fighting For It

I cram it in
wherever I can

meditation before lunch,
a Sunday evening bath,
that cheeky after-work
swim

my mind too
is a battlefield

spiralling out
and often, too chaotic
for me to rally

so, I eat good food
make better choices—
tell myself I am worthy.

I'm not sure
where I stand
on fighting for peace

sure, I deserve it,
but I get so tired
of slotting it into
each crevice
of my soul.

I want it to find me
when I am broken,
daily

into splintered pieces

that need it most,
heal me over
with new skin

blankets draped
across old wounds.

If You've Been Asking For A Sign

do it

treat these words
as indelible ink
tattooing dreams
upon skin

hold your fear
hostage

teach yourself
to run with the wild,
then gift it back
to the page

it howls
your rage in return.

Never Mind The Fish

Twenty was a mess

arriving drenched
in garish spirits
full of cheap beer
and endless
disappointment

clutched itself nightly
before maddening beige
counting each exhale;
a silent death-wish
with no Earthly place
to go.

Thirty was different

it sang about shadows
consuming wild rivers,
found the old Gods
on England's moors

stood open armed
in the ocean to feel
the juice of the world
upon salt-parched lips,
shining out weird beacons
until weirdos howled
in return.

I don't talk
about scars often

how when I shave my legs

I wonder if I trust myself
when cold steel feels
like drunkenness

but I've come to realise
maybe the years themselves
are wounds weeping into hours
as bones attempt to float
amongst a wreck

and the more I allow it

terror
wonder
everything

the more I realise
I am not a number at all

I'm growing gills
swimming through
black time

luminescent space.

This Is Witch-Work

Barefoot at daybreak
feeling a morning
rising through soles
above heavy, wet clay

sipping hemp almond
from a hot brew kept warm
by the sun, as magpies
bow their silent heads

this—
this is witch-work

and it is what I know
of myself and this land
carefully intertwined,
unapologetic

plaiting wild hair beneath moonlight,
savage stars mirroring white eyes
lit up in the knowledge
of Pagan things

speaking a strange language
transcending space & time,
humble enough to lay itself
at my feet

and this—
this is witch-work

the twirl of sacred smoke
from an altar fire
entering the bloodstream

of eternal memory

that is moved by the scent
of lemon balm and rosemary
harvested from a garden
learned to grow in honour
of you.

We're All Just Floating On Through

I swam northward
out across an empty lake
towards the picturesque
village church that towered
its spire above rustling trees

breast-stroke
was effortless
today

a mix of better food
in my belly
and wind in my favour
pushed me across with ease

and I—
I swam
my furthest yet

touched the yellow buoy
anchored on blue rope
above the breakwater

bobbed there
for a good while
letting waves carry me
past perplexed ducks
unsure what type
of fish I was.

There's something

about being out there
with yourself

by
yourself—

you and the deep;
you and God

away from things
that tell you to fear
the world and
everything
in it

I wondered
if birds had
that same feeling.
flying for the first time,
like anything is possible
in an unexplored place

and I feel—
I feel as though
I have swum this way
for a thousand years
circling the stars

birthed myself
entirely in reverse.

Wildling

let it open

      let it consume you—

allow the nectar of words
to drop upon your tongue

remember
their sweetness,
their taste in times
when night is a dark shell
pressed to your ear

and you listen to the howl
of the ocean wash over you

note the cry
of all that is to die
beneath all
that does not serve

then gift it back
to the world

become homeless

set fire to your skin
and paint their cheeks
with your remains

because they—

they are
your stars

mark them
as one of your own.

Acknowledgements

I'd like to thank a few people for their support with this book.

To Ethan, my twin in this life and beautiful friend. I thank you always for your unfailing belief in me as a human being and accepting me exactly as I am. I will always be here for you.

To my Red Tent sisters, who never fail to inspire and uplift me. You make my life so much richer for the experience. I am blessed every day to have you all in my life. Thank you for allowing me to simply be myself.

To Eliza, who patiently listened to all of my ideas to create the perfect artwork for this book cover — thank you for your talent and helping to bring my dreams to reality. It's everything I could have possibly asked for, and more.

To Joe, who never accepted procrastination as an excuse and kicked me regularly into finishing this project, thank you for being a much needed pain in the arse.

To Gabriel and David, who will only ever see this book started in their lifetime from the Otherworld — I hope I made you proud.

To my ex, who taught me exactly the kind of human being I never want to be.

Lastly, to my Husband, my rock, and my biggest fan. There will never be a day where I will not be thankful to the universe for you. Thank you for your support— for seeing something in me worthy of your life, and loving my weird in return.

Gratitude to you all as part of the journey x

L - #0170 - 020222 - C0 - 210/148/9 - PB - DID3260790